John Mark Caton

Words for the Widow

Discovering Your Place and Purpose

Words for the Widow: Discovering Your Place and Purpose
John Mark Caton

Published by Austin Brothers Publishing, Fort Worth, Texas

www.abpbooks.com

ISBN 978-1-7324846-1-0

Copyright © 2018 by John Mark Caton

ALL RIGHTS RESERVED. *No part of this book may be reproduced in any form without permission in writing from the publisher, except in the case of brief quotations embodied in critical reviews or articles.*

Printed in the United States of America

2018 -- First Edition

Jesus saw a poor widow putting in two small copper coins. And He said, "Truly I say to you, this poor widow put in more than all of them...

Contents

A Tribute to My Mom!	1
The Church and Widows	11
Tamar the Tenacious	19
Naomi, Name-Changer	29
Ruth, Risk-Taker	39
Anna, Prophetess and Praise-Giver	47
The Widow's Mite	55
Famine and Feast in Zarephath	63
The Widow from Nain	71

A Tribute to My Mom!

"Many women do noble things, but you surpass them all." (Proverbs 31:29)

My mom, Donnie Caton, was raised in Houston, Texas with her parents Leonard and Hattie Eddings and two wonderful sisters, Novis Lee (Kitty) and Lindell. She grew up working in the family grocery store where at the age of 6, she began restocking the *Coke* cooler with drinks, and by the time she was 13, Mom had worked her way up to serving customers from the front counter. Her tenacious, hard-working spirit helped her balance work and school. She attended Aldine schools all 12 years where she participated in the band, pep squad, and basketball. She was well-liked and was voted Aldine Homecoming Queen in 1953.

After Mom graduated from Aldine High School, she attended the University of Houston where she paid her way through college by continuing to work full-time at the family grocery store for $35 a week. My mom was not "all work and no play;" she also served in several service organizations and enjoyed membership in her sorority, *Alpha Phi*.

The fact that my mom was in a sorority during college was unknown to us until recently. One night we were sitting at the table with our oldest daughter, Jordan, talking about her upcoming sorority rush at the University of Oklahoma. When we asked her which sororities she liked, she mentioned *Alpha Phi*. At that moment, my mother remarked, "I was an *Alpha Phi* at the University of Houston." We were all shocked—we never knew. However, this was characteristic of my mother who almost never talks about herself; her focus is always on others.

In addition to being a hard-worker and socially active, my mother is one of the smartest ladies I know. She graduated from the University of Houston with an Education Degree in History, and English with an additional minor in P.E.

Through it all, her strong faith was and is synonymous with who she is in every way, and it was this faith that in some ways brought her together with her husband. Donnie Caton's faith journey began at age 6 when she would walk herself to church each Sunday. She loved church, and at age 15, she volunteered to teach 8-year-old girls.

While in college, Mom helped organize area revivals, and she interviewed Harlan Caton to preach a revival at her home church. It was love at first "sound" as she fell in love with my father's voice before she ever met him face-to-face. Their first meeting took place on Easter Sunday afternoon when she interviewed him to preach a youth revival. Dad was wearing his new "white-Easter-Suit." (This is the origin of the "white-suit" request Mom makes of me every year at Easter. Just once she wants me to preach a message in a white-suit, white shoes, white socks, white shirt, white tie and even a white vest.)

After that meeting on an April Sunday afternoon, Mom took a risk and invited Harlan out for a first date. Her church had a Sadie Hawkins event to which she invited him. If it was love at first *sound* for my mom, it was love at first *date* for my dad. They dated through the summer months and were married on a Tuesday night in August. Yes, a Tuesday-because that was the only night available between Harlan's previously scheduled revivals.

The newlyweds moved to Marshall, Texas, so that Dad could attend East Texas Baptist College. While they were in East Texas, they had their first two children Kathy and James. My mom began her teaching career in Karnack while my dad began preaching at a small, local church and driving a school bus. These were challenging but fun times as the Karnack teaching position required many long hours in addition to the time demand of ministering alongside her husband in the church. Mom recounted a story of her first Sunday with this new congregation as she upset the members because she sat on the *wrong side* of the church. This was her first of many life-lessons about the harshness, silliness, and stubbornness of many church members.

After that first Sunday, the men of the church called my dad aside and told him that his wife had sat on the wrong side of the worship center—Strike One. Not long after that those same men called my dad aside after a sermon and said—we don't want you preaching against drinking and smoking anymore—Strike Two. The last straw came when after a Sunday morning service, those same men called my father aside and chastised him for inviting the wrong kind of people to the church—people they didn't like—Strike three.

The next Sunday, my mother and father drove to church, and Dad backed the car into a parking space. Dad preached as usual, and at that time mom sat in the back of the church with her two young children Kathy and James. After preaching a rather abrasive sermon to the church, my dad resigned on the spot with the announcement that he wouldn't be back. His departing word for the congregation was "Ichabod" which means the "glory has departed."

After resigning, Harlan Caton walked down the center aisle, and my parents walked out the back door. As they drove off, Mom asked, "When did you decide to resign?" He said, "On the way to church this morning." They drove off without a job, but they were happy not to be going back.

The couple had many good and bad memories from these early times. Not all churches are good churches, and not all church members are good people. But as with everything in Mom's life, she never let one bad apple spoil the whole bunch.

As soon as Harlan finished his degree at East Texas Baptist College, they left Marshall and accepted an invitation to pastor Spring Baptist Church in Spring, Texas. They began their ministry on July 1, 1962, with about 75 church members. Shortly after starting ministry in Spring, I was born. Mom taught junior high school for 25 years in Spring ISD. Her marriage was filled with spontaneous moments and memories of trips, funny stories, God-moments, and both laughter and pain.

Because of Dad's passion for God's Word, endless energy, and decisive leadership, Spring Baptist Church began to grow almost immediately. But regardless of how well the church was doing, pastors and their families live in the proverbial "Fish-Bowl." Mom recounts when people in the church would occasionally point a finger at a Caton child.

What most people didn't know about my dad is that he grew up the son of an abusive alcoholic and had to fight for survival from an early age both inside and outside the home. His salvation experience changed him in many ways spiritually and directed that unbridled passion to God and His people. When it came to my dad if you wanted to talk about God's Word, the church, reaching people for Christ, or mission, you got Pastor Caton. However, when you began to speak negatively about his family, you didn't get Pastor Caton you got Harlan.

Again, my mom never let one bad apple spoil the whole bunch. She loved her husband, her family, and her church. She loved that Harlan could always make up his mind, and he never backed down from a conviction. He prayed about every decision. She still describes him as "the best preacher in the world!" She liked being a part of Harlan's ministry and being by his side. She loved her husband's passion for people, hunger for knowing God's Word, and his constant desire to have fun.

Mom noted that just like the resignation at the first church Dad was prone to make quick, decisive decisions… sometimes consulting her and sometimes not. It was not uncommon for Dad to mention a boat in one sentence, and then the next thing Mom knew, there was a boat in the driveway. When she would ask him about it, he would usually say, "It will be fun!" Most of the time that was true, but when he drove home on a motorcycle one day Mom was not happy, and she did not see the fun.

Before my father passed away, the church continued to grow and reach people. God provided during this time. When Dad died at age 50, my parents had ministered at Spring for 23 years. Many lives had been mentored, ministered to, and eternally changed. Spring Baptist was an influential church in the area and one of the very few campuses that could claim to be completely debt-free due to God's provisions through faithful members and strong leadership.

After my father passed away, Mom missed him being by her side. She missed his conversation, his preaching, his cooking, and his decisive decision-making. She still misses him to this day and has never remarried because no other man has ever caught her eye like Harlan Caton did. However, as much as she misses my dad, she chose NOT to become bitter. Instead, she did what she had always done... poured herself into her career, her family, and her service to God in the church.

Yes, even today after all these years she asks God if He made a mistake taking her husband so young, and although she still doesn't have the answer, she has not stopped making her mark for God's Kingdom. She has not stopped loving and investing in her friends and family. She carries on as a strong, independent woman.

After my father passed away, my mother has faced some tough challenges. My brother, James, constantly struggled. He was handsome, athletic, and funny, but there was the other side of James that demonstrated a hot-head, anger, and bitterness. If you wanted a fight, he was willing to oblige, but it probably wasn't going to turn out well for you. Like so many others, James always struggled to find his place in life. As a result, he suffered with depression and turned to alcohol to numb the pain of a lost marriage, loneliness, and a difficult path.

When he was losing his battle to the addiction, out of misplaced respect for his family, he often isolated himself and issues would go from bad to worse. However, when James came to a place of hopelessness, he made the choice to end his life far too soon.

This was a tough time for my mom, but she knew better than anyone that isolation is never the answer to a problem and loneliness never heals a wound. Mom is a cornerstone for her family. She is ALWAYS there for her children, grandchildren, great-grandchildren, sisters, and friends. She has spent countless hours on the sidelines watching her kids and grandkids do what they love. Neither, the sweltering Texas heat, the driving rain, Dallas wind, nor freezing weather can keep her from being where she wants to be supporting her family.

Mom is a strong, smart, independent woman. She is part of an active group at Spring Baptist called *The Classics*. This group fellowships, travels, and provides friendships. She loves the fact that her church actively honors and cares for all widows in the congregation. God has sustained her and cared for her over the years. God has been her comfort when she was sad and her peace to get through every day. She has learned to let God guide her through a faithful prayer life, She trusts God completely, and she seeks and patiently waits on God.

Her life loudly resounds with strength and positivity, and she expects nothing less from those around her. Mom is tenacious about life in every way, and she doesn't have much patience for whiners and complainers. It is almost as if her life motto is, "Whiners don't win, and complainers don't make good companions." If you need someone to give you a word of encouragement, lend you a helping hand, or pray with you, Mom is there for you. However, if you just want to sit around and whine and complain about life, bad circumstances, and other people, she doesn't have much time for that—that's a dead-end road and Mom isn't a fan of dead-end roads because she has places to go and people to see.

She is in her mid-80s now, but on any given Sunday, it is pretty easy to find her. She will be at the church she loves looking for someone to serve not expecting someone to serve her. Every Sunday she arrives at church early to take her place at the Welcome Center to distribute bulletins, chat with old friends, and welcome new guests and help them find their way around the church. And when she is finished handing out bulletins, she will go to her class, open her well-worn Bible, and teach. She has been a teacher at Spring Baptist for over 50 years.

When asked what advice she would give to a new widow, she responded, "Take all your problems to God. Go to your family for advice and use friends and family as a sounding board."

For Mom, being a widow is not synonymous with bitterness and loneliness. Bitterness is a choice a person makes after a tough season in life. While bitterness may seem to be a natural outcome of being a widow and losing a son, Mom knows that the fruit of bitterness is rotten to its core. And, as for loneliness, that is a choice too. You can choose to isolate yourself, throw a pity party and spend your time alone—or you can choose to pour your life into others which is really why God put us all here to begin with.

I Love You Mom and gain strength and wisdom by watching your example every day!

John Mark

The Church and Widows

In those days when the number of disciples was increasing, the Hellenistic Jews among them complained against the Hebraic Jews because their widows were being overlooked in the daily distribution of food. So the Twelve gathered all the disciples together and said, "It would not be right for us to neglect the ministry of the word of God in order to wait on tables. Brothers and sisters, choose seven men from among you who are known to be full of the Spirit and wisdom. We will turn this responsibility over to them and will give our attention to prayer and the ministry of the word."

This proposal pleased the whole group. They chose Stephen, a man full of faith and of the Holy Spirit; also Philip, Procorus, Nicanor, Timon, Parmenas, and Nicolas from Antioch, a convert to Judaism. They presented these men to the apostles, who prayed and laid their hands on them.

So the word of God spread. The number of disciples in Jerusalem increased rapidly, and a large number of priests became obedient to the faith. (Acts 6:1-7)

It's highly likely that a book on the subject of the church and widows will begin by quoting Acts 6 and this one is no exception. Most people point to that account as an example of how the church appointed Deacons to minister to the needs of widows. However, this book is not just about Deacons. It describes a priority of the church.

The Pentecost awakening and subsequent massive number of new followers of Christ threw the community into chaos. Suddenly, eleven disciples with perhaps a few hundred true followers of Jesus were faced with the reality of thousands of new followers. Imagine the chaos if your church had a customary attendance of one hundred on Sunday morning had three thousand new converts show up next Sunday. Obviously, there would be much to do.

In the case of the early church as described in the book of Acts, one of those issues concerned widows. The church was doing its best to take care of their needs, but there was some background noise from the Greeks that their widows were being overlooked in favor of the Hebrew widows. We don't know how many widows were involved, but the issue was deemed important enough to engage the Twelve in finding a solution.

Before we dive into a discussion of the church's concern for widows, let's take a moment to reflect on what we understand by the term "widow." The primary meaning of the word is a woman whose husband has died. Perhaps he died when they were still young or maybe it was after fifty plus years of marriage. Often, our first thought with the mention of the term is an elderly woman who struggles to survive.

That image indeed encompasses a large number of widows, but there are also widows who are financially secure and healthy enough to travel and enjoy many of the finer things of life. Some of the most significant philanthropists are widows. Laurene Powell Jobs, widow of Steve Jobs of Apple computer fame has given away millions of dollars to various organizations. Other widows take over control of successful businesses and are able to continue the success.

Another group of widows is those who have children who are willing and able to take care of their mother. They spent their life caring for and providing for the family and now that they are in the later stages of life, they are on the receiving end of care provided by the family. It's safe to say that a healthy sign of a culture is the way they handle the elderly.

There are also many widows who achieved that status while still young. Perhaps their husband died in an accident or was a casualty of war or suffered a fatal disease. They are young enough to work and provide for themselves. Often, they have young children who are left without a father.

Every widow has a unique story and situation. However, the church has always recognized an obligation to treat these women according to the attitude God has toward them.

Since the beginning of recorded history, being a widow typically meant a struggle for survival. Most ancient cultures, especially the Hebrew culture described in the Old Testament, were focused on men. Men possessed privileges and opportunities that women did not have. Marriage served several purposes, the least of which was companionship. People got married for the sake of survival.

Men needed women in order to procreate. Women needed men to have food and shelter. If they happened to genuinely love each other, that was a special, extra benefit. The man provided for the family as a whole, and the woman made sure the individual needs were met out of the man's provision.

When the man died for some reason, the family was thrown into chaos. If he had sons, then they would be expected to take up the slack. However, if he did not have any sons or if the ones he had were too young, then the widow was left on her own. The Old Testament did prescribe a process for the extended family members to adopt the widow as part of their family, but this system was not always practical.

If a widow did not have independent wealth or a family to provide her needs, she was left to the life of a beggar. We often find her classified with orphans as the two types of people who were to be most pitied. Remember, in ancient days, women did not have the opportunity to simply get a job and make a living on their own. To do such was a rare occurrence.

God takes the care of these defenseless people very seriously. Time after time, He instructed His people to be sure to take care of them. Helping widows was woven into the fabric of God's people. We even find this in the ministry of Jesus. One of the people he raised from the dead was the son of a widow. In doing so, he not only restored life to the young man, but He also expressed grace to the widow who would have been destitute without her son.

The early church described in the Book of Acts was born into that world. Taking care of widows among them would have been a natural thing. They were doing just that when a problem arose. Some felt certain ethnic widows were being favored over others. The Twelve, who thought it unwise to neglect their preaching to resolve this issue, chose to set aside a group of seven men to take on this responsibility.

An interesting side note is that the names of the seven chosen suggest they were all Hellenistic. Perhaps it was thought they would be the ones most likely to make sure the Hellenistic widows were provided for.

Historically, the selection of these seven men has been considered the beginning of the concept of Deacons within the church. The word "deacon" is not mentioned in this passage but the fact that the origin of the word means "servant" then it is a natural assumption. These men were chosen to be servants, or "wait on tables" as the passage indicates. In their case, the primary recipients of their service were widows.

This same attitude of concern for widows was expressed later in the writings of the early church.

Give proper recognition to those widows who are really in need. But if a widow has children or grandchildren, these should learn first of all to put their religion into practice by caring for their own family and so repaying their parents and grandparents, for this is pleasing to God. The widow who is really in need and left all alone puts her hope in God and continues night and day to pray and to ask God for help. But the widow who lives for pleasure is dead even while she lives. Give the people these instructions, so that no one may be open to blame. Anyone who does not provide for their relatives, and especially for their own household, has denied the faith and is worse than an unbeliever. (1 Timothy 5:3-8)

Beginning with this event in Jerusalem, historically the church has taken on the responsibility of tending to the needs of widows in the congregation. Even today, many churches have organized programs that not only include providing financial considerations, but also assistance with chores like house and auto repairs, transportation, and companionship/friendship.

However, just because a woman has lost her husband, her value to the Kingdom of God has not been lessened.

A Ministry for Widows

Likewise, teach the older women to be reverent in the way they live, not to be slanderers or addicted to much wine, but to teach what is good. Then they can urge the younger women to love their husbands and children, to be self-controlled and pure, to be busy at home, to be kind, and to be subject to their husbands, so that no one will malign the word of God. (Titus 2:3-5)

With these words, Paul instructs Titus to encourage the older widows to teach the younger women. There is tremendous value in experience that can only be taught by older women. The practical aspects of this truth are significant. They can offer encouragement, friendship, and advice in the midst of struggles. It is vital for widows to make themselves available for this important ministry.

The Leadership of Widows

As Jesus looked up, he saw the rich putting their gifts into the temple treasury. He also saw a poor widow put in two very small copper coins. "Truly I tell you," he said, "this poor widow has put in more than all the others. All these people gave their gifts out of their wealth; but she out of her poverty put in all she had to live on." (Luke 21:1-4)

We'll meet this particular widow later in the book but let me simply mention now that she provides a powerful example of the leadership a widow can be. Jesus specifically pointed her out to His disciples and said she is the example to follow. In fact, her action has been instructive to believers throughout the entire history of the church.

Widows fill an essential role in the work of Christ in the world. The church has always recognized this truth, and the purpose of this book is to remind these women of their value. Each chapter is like viewing a valuable jewel from a different angle. Each profile contains its own beauty, but when taken together, there is no mistaking the truth that widows play a particular role in God's plan for the world.

Tamar the Tenacious

God is Faithful When Man Fails

Judah got a wife for Er, his firstborn, and her name was Tamar. But Er, Judah's firstborn, was wicked in the Lord's sight; so the Lord put him to death.

Then Judah said to Onan, "Sleep with your brother's wife and fulfill your duty to her as a brother-in-law to raise up offspring for your brother." But Onan knew that the child would not be his; so whenever he slept with his brother's wife, he spilled his semen on the ground to keep from providing offspring for his brother. What he did was wicked in the Lord's sight; so the Lord put him to death also.

Judah then said to his daughter-in-law Tamar, "Live as a widow in your father's household until my son Shelah grows up." For he thought, "He may die too, just like his brothers." So Tamar went to live in her father's household.

After a long time Judah's wife, the daughter of Shua, died. When Judah had recovered from his grief, he went up to Timnah, to the men who were shearing his sheep, and his friend Hirah the Adullamite went with him.

When Tamar was told, "Your father-in-law is on his way to Timnah to shear his sheep," she took off her widow's clothes, covered herself with a veil to disguise herself, and then sat down at the entrance to Enaim, which is on the road to Timnah. For she saw that, though Shelah had now grown up, she had not been given to him as his wife.

When Judah saw her, he thought she was a prostitute, for she had covered her face. Not realizing that she was his daughter-in-law, he went over to her by the roadside and said, "Come now, let me sleep with you."

"And what will you give me to sleep with you?" she asked.

"I'll send you a young goat from my flock," he said.

"Will you give me something as a pledge until you send it?" she asked.

He said, "What pledge should I give you?"

"Your seal and its cord, and the staff in your hand," she answered. So he gave them to her and slept with her, and she became pregnant by him. After she left, she took off her veil and put on her widow's clothes again.

Meanwhile Judah sent the young goat by his friend the Adullamite in order to get his pledge back from the woman, but he did not find her. He asked the men who lived there, "Where is the shrine prostitute who was beside the road at Enaim?"

"There hasn't been any shrine prostitute here," they said.

So he went back to Judah and said, "I didn't find her. Besides, the men who lived there said, 'There hasn't been any shrine prostitute here.'"

Then Judah said, "Let her keep what she has, or we will become a laughingstock. After all, I did send her this young goat, but you didn't find her."

About three months later Judah was told, "Your daughter-in-law Tamar is guilty of prostitution, and as a result she is now pregnant."

Judah said, "Bring her out and have her burned to death!"

As she was being brought out, she sent a message to her father-in-law. "I am pregnant by the man who owns these," she said. And she added, "See if you recognize whose seal and cord and staff these are."

Judah recognized them and said, "She is more righteous than I, since I wouldn't give her to my son Shelah." And he did not sleep with her again.

When the time came for her to give birth, there were twin boys in her womb. As she was giving birth, one of them put out his hand; so the midwife took a scarlet thread and tied it on his wrist and said, "This one came out first." But when he drew back his hand, his brother came out, and she said, "So this is how you have broken out!" And he was named Perez. Then his brother, who had the scarlet thread on his wrist, came out. And he was named Zerah. (Genesis 38:6-30)

We read much in this passage that may shock and confuse. A widow, Tamar, who should have been cared for by the family into which she had married, is neglected and rejected by those who should have protected and honored her. This is not a passage we usually equate with encouragement because there are many messy details in the story. But often, being a widow involves some unpleasant details. Some widows are young, and some are old, some widows have great relatives, and others do not, and some widows have children who care for them while others do not.

Regardless of the details, one thing is abundantly clear—Tamar is Tenacious. That word tenacious means to hold fast or to be persistent. Tamar is all of that and more. She refuses to quit and is willing to do whatever it takes to find justice for herself.

Research the Information...

In ancient times, wealth was tied to the land. Men were needed for such backbreaking and strenuous work. Sons were celebrated, and the highest portion of the inheritance (land) went to the oldest son.

In this historical setting, women were dependent on men who would use their strength to care for them and allow them to flourish. If men of the family did not utilize that strength to the service of the women, especially a widow, they would fall into the margins of society, fail to thrive and struggle to even survive.

In Tamar's story, we read that Tamar's husband was a wicked man and unfaithful to the Lord. Strike one, Team Judah. As the widow of the firstborn son, Tamar should have been shown honor. More than that, she would have continued to desire to show honor to her husband's lineage.

A family custom of producing an heir for the deceased brother and caring for his widow should have been observed. It was a tall order: the second son would have been set to inherit everything! This custom, which focused on provisions for the widow and the continuation of the family name, was formalized into Judaic law (see Deuteronomy 25:5-9).

In Tamar's case, we see that laying aside his concerns for the sake of another was more than Onan could bear. Onan's unfaithfulness is his downfall: Strike two for the men of Judah. Judah completes the cycle of mistreatment and neglect, sending Tamar back to her father's household with nothing more than empty hands and empty promises. Strike three, Judah.

At this pivotal moment, we must think about what we know of the line of Judah. From the benefit of where we stand in redemptive history, we know that Jesus came from Judah, as Jacob prophesied in Genesis 49, and as can be seen later in Matthew's genealogy: "Abraham was the father of Isaac, and Isaac the father of Jacob, and Jacob the father of Judah and his brothers, and Judah the father of Perez and Zerah by Tamar..."

Right there, smack in the middle of the genealogical litany of Judah and Tamar, his infamy is written in large letters for all the world to see. An allusion to his unfaithful behavior is clearly included in the lineage of our precious Savior and Lord–another example of God's faithfulness in the face of man's failure.

We've saved the best "deep look" for last: Tamar was not even a woman of Israel, but a Canaanite and it only gets worse. Her husband was an evil man; she was widowed, mistreated by both brother-in-law and father-in-law...and yet, she tenaciously clung to her sense of what was right, seeking after it with all her might.

What do we see in Tamar's Story? We recognize that God was overseeing all of Tamar's experiences and troubles: and He was for her even when others were not.

What, then, shall we say in response to these things? If God is for us, who can be against us? (Romans 8:31)

The Lord honored Tamar's noble quest even when the details were messy, and others who should have cared for her rejected her. God gave her a significant place in His chosen family: Israel. But God didn't stop there—the Father was pursuing His magnificent redemptive plan, consummated in sending His Son to provide for those lost in their sinfulness, shame, and sad circumstances. He has woven Tamar's story into The Story—His Story! God makes Tamar an ancestress to the promised Messiah: our Savior and Lord, Jesus Christ. What greater honor and privilege!

He lifted me out of the slimy pit, out of the mud and mire; he set my feet on a rock and gave me a firm place to stand. (Psalm 40:2)

Recognize the Implication...

Tamar knew with every fiber of her being what the righteous way of dealing with a widow and her late husband's legacy ought to be, and she fought for it with all her might. Her pursuit of justice won her a place in the Hall of Faith—Tamar was Tenacious!

You have the great benefit of standing on the other side of so much redemptive history from Tamar's story. You can read the God-inspired writings that teach us the way of loving (Him and neighbor), and you can reflect on the promises given to men and women—even men like Judah! Every one of these promises was fulfilled in the person of Jesus Christ and revealed through the words of the apostles.

So, if you find yourself abandoned and failed by those who should care for and love you—pursue God and be confident in His faithfulness toward you! God is there for you even when others are not.

"Be strong and courageous. Do not be afraid or terrified because of them, for the Lord your God goes with you; he will never leave you nor forsake you." (Deuteronomy 31:6)

REFLECT ON THE APPLICATION

In your widowhood, maybe you have felt neglected and rejected by those who should have loved and cared for you. How does the story of Tamar encourage you to use your intelligence and resourcefulness to thrive in the world your Heavenly Father has made?

How might your pursuit of righteousness and justice, like Tamar's, play into the greater story of God's redemption? Let that thought motivate you as you engage all that the Lord has for you today!

Further study: Read Isaiah 61; focus mainly on verses 7-11, where the prophet beautifully explores the themes of God's justice, righteousness, and blessing, just as we have investigated them today through the story of Tamar. Claim these words for your own as you meet with your Heavenly Father, today.

Naomi, Name-Changer

God is Big Enough to Handle our Bitterness

In the days when the judges ruled, there was a famine in the land. So a man from Bethlehem in Judah, together with his wife and two sons, went to live for a while in the country of Moab. The man's name was Elimelek, his wife's name was Naomi, and the names of his two sons were Mahlon and Kilion. They were Ephrathites from Bethlehem, Judah. And they went to Moab and lived there.

Now Elimelek, Naomi's husband, died, and she was left with her two sons. They married Moabite women, one named Orpah and the other Ruth. After they had lived there about ten years, both Mahlon and Kilion also died, and Naomi was left without her two sons and her husband.

Naomi and Ruth Return to Bethlehem

When Naomi heard in Moab that the Lord had come to the aid of his people by providing food for them, she and her daughters-in-law prepared to return home from there. With her two daughters-in-law she left the place where she had been living and set out on the road that would take them back to the land of Judah.

Then Naomi said to her two daughters-in-law, "Go back, each of you, to your mother's home. May the Lord show you kindness, as you have shown kindness to your dead husbands and to me. May the Lord grant that each of you will find rest in the home of another husband."

Then she kissed them goodbye and they wept aloud and said to her, "We will go back with you to your people."

But Naomi said, "Return home, my daughters. Why would you come with me? Am I going to have any more sons, who could become your husbands? Return home, my daughters; I am too old to have another husband. Even if I thought there was still hope for me—even if I had a husband tonight and then gave birth to sons—would you wait until they grew up? Would you remain unmarried for them? No, my daughters.

It is more bitter for me than for you, because the Lord's hand has turned against me!"

At this they wept aloud again. Then Orpah kissed her mother-in-law goodbye, but Ruth clung to her.

"Look," said Naomi, "your sister-in-law is going back to her people and her gods. Go back with her."

But Ruth replied, "Don't urge me to leave you or to turn back from you. Where you go I will go, and where you stay I will stay. Your people will be my people and your God my God. Where you die I will die, and there I will be buried. May the Lord deal with me, be it ever so severely, if even death separates you and me." When Naomi realized that Ruth was determined to go with her, she stopped urging her.

So the two women went on until they came to Bethlehem. When they arrived in Bethlehem, the whole town was stirred because of them, and the women exclaimed, "Can this be Naomi?"

"Don't call me Naomi," she told them. "Call me Mara, because the Almighty has made my life very bitter. I went away full, but the Lord has brought me back empty. Why call me Naomi? The Lord has afflicted me; the Almighty has brought misfortune upon me." (Ruth 1:1-21)

Naomi's story goes from bad to worse in just a few verses—from famine in Israel to the death of her husband, Elimelech. Unfortunately for Naomi and her daughters-in-law, it doesn't stop there. The bitterest pill is left to swallow yet when both of her sons die. The loss of children is said to be the most grievous loss of all. But in Naomi's day, her sons would have been tasked with the responsibility of supplying her material needs in the present as well as securing her and her deceased husband's future legacy.

As a result, Naomi is left "alone" with her daughters-in-law in a foreign land. It is no wonder that she changes her name from "Pleasant" to "Bitter." Years earlier it was Naomi which means pleasant, who had left family and friends in Bethlehem with her husband for a new land and a brighter future. Now it is Mara which means bitter, not Naomi who returns to Bethlehem.

"...weeping may stay for the night, but rejoicing comes in the morning." (Psalm 30:5)

Research the Information...

Our familiarity with the book of Ruth causes us to want to move quickly through the discomfort and difficulties of the opening chapter of the book in order to see the happy ending. We want to read about Naomi's burdens lifted, and her empty hands filled once more with a child of her family's kinsman redeemer. We want to rush to the hope and the promise that a better Redeemer is coming—Jesus Christ!

The beauty of the concluding chapter of the book of Ruth is that it seems to set things right and gives us a sense of meaning and fulfillment. It calls to our remembrance the treasured truth in God's Word that God works all things together for the good of those who love Him.

"And we know that in all things God works for the good of those who love him, who have been called according to his purpose."(Romans 8:28)

However, to move too quickly to the end of the story and not grapple with the tough part at the start, ignores a reality we know all too well. We live in a painful and sinful world, and significant setbacks and heartbreaks are not overcome in a couple of chapters. In the midst of those tough seasons in life, it is difficult, if not impossible, to embrace the happy ending let alone even consider a happy ending possible.

Naomi's pleasant life had been filled with hope and promise, but much like Job, it was taken away. The relational blessing of being a wife, the maternal blessing of being a mother, and the matriarchal blessing of being a mother-in-law were taken away in an instant. Life was cruel to Naomi, and the material blessings of her life were stripped away, and she was left with next to nothing!

Naomi and her husband had worked to overcome the difficulties of the famine, but these physical preparations failed to grant Naomi security and fell short of protecting her from loss, pain, and devastation. Naomi, like so many of us, had perhaps believed in the Lord's sovereignty in her mind, while doing everything in her power to physically control her circumstances. In her grief, she lays the blame, not once, not twice, not even three times at the Lord's feet. Naomi names her grievances against the Lord four times, reflecting the depth of her bitterness and distress.

Not only this, but she changes her own name, which is akin to changing her identity. Consider the people in the Bible whose names are changed by God or some other authority: "Sarai" (my princess) is changed to "Sarah" (mother of nations); Jacob, ("supplanter") is changed to "Israel," which means "having power with God;" Daniel and his fellow Hebrews have their names changed by order of King Nebuchadnezzar to Babylonian names in order to assimilate them into his kingdom. Abram to Abraham. Saul to Paul. All these name changes mark a significant change in the story.

What kind of self-talk can you imagine of this newly-embittered "Mara?" It is often said that "we listen to ourselves more than anyone else." There is more truth in that statement than most of us are willing to admit, but the truth is what we say to ourselves reverberates through our minds, hearts, and emotions. When things got quiet, did Naomi beat herself up, or blame herself for having left Israel for a foreign land? Did she blame her deceased husband? Did her self-talk impact Naomi's belief in God's love and purpose for her life?

Or perhaps, as I would like to think, Naomi was coming to the only Father she knew: like a child; full of all of her emotions, unable to clean herself up or pretend everything was going to be "okay." Maybe, even though she didn't understand why her story was unfolding so bitterly, she knew that God was ultimately in charge of her situation and because of that she still had hope for a better future.

"For I know the plans I have for you," declares the Lord, "plans to prosper you and not to harm you, plans to give you hope and a future." (Jeremiah 29:11)

We cannot know for sure the real state of her faith at this point. But what we can observe is God's immediate provision, first in Ruth, then in old friends, later in Boaz, and finally in her grandson, Obed. The Lord does not leave her in her bitterness, nor does He discipline her for it! Naomi's Heavenly Father ministers to her in her grief, changing her identity once more, this time from Bitter and Empty to Loved and Full!

"Praise be to the God and Father of our Lord Jesus Christ, the Father of compassion and the God of all comfort, who comforts us in all our troubles, so that we can comfort those in any trouble with the comfort we ourselves receive from God. For just as we share abundantly in the sufferings of Christ, so also our comfort abounds through Christ." (2 Corinthians 1:3-5)

Recognize the Implication...

Perhaps the grief of your loss has weighed heavily on you—heavily enough to change your personality or to make you question your very identity. Maybe where you were once outgoing, you are now shy or reserved; maybe where you once took delight in everything, you now protect your heart from more disappointment, and maybe where you were once full of trust in God and others, you now wrestle with doubt.

In this season, in these moments of struggle when the emotional tides come crashing in, perhaps what you need to hear the most is: I know your heart; I hear your pain; I am big enough to hear it and take it all. I AM.

Naomi turned to the Only One who could handle her heart: the One who made it. She didn't understand, she couldn't fix it, she had doubts that anyone else could, either. And the Lord met her there. He doesn't require that we clean ourselves up before we come to Him.

"Come to me, all you who are weary and burdened, and I will give you rest. Take my yoke upon you and learn from me, for I am gentle and humble in heart, and you will find rest for your souls." (Matthew 11:28-29, NLT)

The One who said this is the same yesterday, today, and forever (Hebrews 13:8). Go to Him now with all of your heart's emotions, with all of your mind's questions, with all of your body's weariness. Recognize the Implication of our Heavenly Father's overwhelming love and care for you and find rest for your soul.

Reflect on the Application...

Naomi, in her bitterness, almost missed the way that Ruth reached out to her in love. Where, how, and through whom has the Lord displayed His love to you? Allow others to love you, receiving with gratitude the grace He has provided you through them. Don't let yourself be bitter and critical of others who don't or cannot meet all your needs.

The story the Lord has written for you, every single moment of your life, is written for your good and His glory. What is more, your story is a part of His Great Story of Redemption! What words, from this passage or others, do you need to dwell in today to bolster your hope? Journal them; work to memorize them; allow them to speak life and peace to you in this season.

Further study: Read Psalm 30. In today's story, Naomi is filled with despair—the "dark night of the soul." The psalmist—King David, the grandson of Obed—reminds us that "though weeping may last for the night, joy comes in the morning." This is the promise of our salvation: He will come to us! (John 14:18b).

Ruth, Risk-Taker

God's Love Motivates Loving Servanthood

Ruth the Moabite said to Naomi, "Let me go to the fields and pick up the leftover grain behind anyone in whose eyes I find favor."

Naomi said to her, "Go ahead, my daughter." So she went out, entered a field and began to glean behind the harvesters. As it turned out, she was working in a field belonging to Boaz, who was from the clan of Elimelek.

Just then Boaz arrived from Bethlehem and greeted the harvesters, "The Lord be with you!"

"The Lord bless you!" they answered.

Boaz asked the overseer of his harvesters, "Who does that young woman belong to?"

The overseer replied, "She is the Moabite who came back from Moab with Naomi. She said, 'Please let me glean and gather among the sheaves behind the harvesters.' She came into the field and has remained here from morning till now, except for a short rest in the shelter."

So Boaz said to Ruth, "My daughter, listen to me. Don't go and glean in another field and don't go away from here. Stay here with the women who work for me. Watch the field where the men are harvesting, and follow along after the women. I have told the men not to lay a hand on you. And whenever you are thirsty, go and get a drink from the water jars the men have filled."

At this, she bowed down with her face to the ground. She asked him, "Why have I found such favor in your eyes that you notice me—a foreigner?"

Boaz replied, "I've been told all about what you have done for your mother-in-law since the death of your husband—how you left your father and mother and your homeland and came to live with a people you did not know before. May the Lord repay you for what you have done. May you be richly rewarded by the Lord, the God of Israel, under whose wings you have come to take refuge." (Ruth 2:2-12)

The entire book of Ruth narrates a rich story in five chapters—a story in the running for "best romance" of the Old Testament. But Ruth's story is not a "romance," like we think of in the movies—not a romance of boy meets girl, they fall in love and live happily ever after. No, this is a story of heartache, self-sacrifice, and heroism mingled with God's provision, human responsibility, and the harvest of righteousness and loving-kindness.

However, none of this goodness happens if Ruth had not taken a risk. That word risk means to expose oneself to danger or potential loss, and that is precisely what Ruth does. She leaves the familiar people and land from her youth for the people of God and God Himself. The reward for such a godly risk makes the story of Ruth so beautiful.

"But Ruth replied, "Don't urge me to leave you or to turn back from you. Where you go I will go, and where you stay I will stay. Your people will be my people and your God my God. Where you die I will die, and there I will be buried. May the Lord deal with me, be it ever so severely, if even death separates you and me." (Ruth 1:16-17)

Research the Information...

If you are familiar with the story of Ruth, you will remember that her mother-in-law Naomi and her husband, Elimelech left for Moab to flee famine in Israel. Ruth and Orpah were Moabite women who married Naomi's two sons. Unfortunately, not only did Elimelech die, but Naomi's two sons also passed away ten years later, leaving all three women widowed—Naomi, Ruth, and Orpah.

Think of all that could have happened during these ten years. Ruth had probably settled into her new life with her husband and mother-in-law. Usually, the first decade of marriage would have seen the birth of children and daily routines would have been established. For some reason or another, Ruth was left childless, increasing the grief over the loss of their husband. Naomi, Ruth, and Orpah were left empty-handed and empty-hearted.

During the grieving period, Ruth and Orpah accompanied Naomi as she journeyed back to her homeland, seeking to honor both her and their late husbands. However, Ruth's mother-in-law Naomi confronted them on the journey and explained the bitter predicament of their situation.

Naomi was returning to her people, yes, but she had nothing to offer the younger women: no home, no close kin, no promise of provision for them in Israel. Furthermore, since Ruth and Orpah were Moabites, it was possible or even likely that the two Moabite women would be shunned and ostracized from God's people because of a history of bad blood between Israelites and Moabites.

"No Ammonite or Moabite or any of their descendants may enter the assembly of the Lord, not even in the tenth generation. For they did not come to meet you with bread and water on your way when you came out of Egypt, and

they hired Balaam son of Beor from Pethor in Aram Naharaim to pronounce a curse on you. (Deuteronomy 23:3-4)

Ruth had developed a profound love for her mother-in-law and was deeply attached to her and refused to leave. This love motivated Ruth to forsake her Moabite people, her land, her gods, and all the possibilities of future comfort through remarriage to follow her beloved mother-in-law Naomi and the God of Naomi's people. Orpah, however, chose differently and went back to her Moabite people and homeland, and her decision should make us pause and reflect. What was different about Ruth that caused her to stay with Naomi when Orpah would not? Ruth was a Risk-Taker!

Ruth's love for Naomi was more than a matter of human affection. Think of what Ruth faced: no promise of a husband, comfort, or familiar culture; a "bitter," aging, and needy mother-in-law with no means to provide for herself, much less for Ruth, and hard labor in the hot sun for survival. These were the conditions Ruth faced when she made her commitment to Naomi, and she made her commitment in spite of these challenges. It was a risky move with the prospect of discomfort, isolation, and possibly even death.

Without God at work in her life, she too might have chosen Orpah's path away from God. But we know Ruth's story because she made a brave decision. Only a heart strengthened by God's supernatural power, presence, and pursuing-love could choose such a path of risk and self-sacrifice. Ruth's heart had been transformed and motivated by God's faithfulness to love and serve her mother-in-law.

In the passage above, we see that the Lord's blessings begin to unfold. God had a plan for Ruth's life all along, beginning with a man who covered her with his cloak. Boaz, a faithful and humble man of God, accepted the call to act as kinsman-redeemer—one who helps restore a disadvantaged family member. Their union is witnessed by the people who bless them saying "May you prosper in Ephrathah and be famous in Bethlehem. And may the Lord give you descendants by this young woman who will be like those of our ancestor Perez, the son of Tamar and Judah" (Ruth 4:11b-12).

Sure enough, the union of Boaz and Ruth produces fruit: a son, Obed, whose name means "servant" and who was a blessing to his grandmother, Naomi. But not only that, the blessing that began Ruth's service to her mother-in-law, Naomi, was extended through Obed to all of Israel, for he was a grandfather to King David. Ruth's willingness to love and serve God and mother-in-law faithfully in ordinary ways bore extraordinary results. As a result, Ruth the Moabite was brought into the family of God and ultimately into the family of Christ, the kinsman-redeemer of the world.

"...an angel of the Lord appeared to him in a dream and said, "Joseph son of David, do not be afraid to take Mary home as your wife, because what is conceived in her is from the Holy Spirit. She will give birth to a son, and you are to

give him the name Jesus, because he will save his people from their sins." (Matthew 1:20-21)

Recognize the Implication...

Did you notice the blessing that Boaz spoke over Ruth at the end of the story? He asked that the Lord would "reward her fully" for what she had done. Boaz saw Ruth's care of her mother-in-law and the risk she had taken by leaving all she had known. In Ruth, Boaz saw a woman transformed by the Lord into a servant. Because Ruth chose to follow God by being a servant to someone else (Naomi) instead of being downcast by her situation, she was not only restored from widow to wife, but she was also given the gift of a child. Not only was she redeemed by a kinsman-redeemer, but she, Ruth, a Gentile, was made an ancestress to her Redeemer: Jesus Christ.

God delights in you just as He delighted in Ruth! God has a plan for your life, and it does not include merely sitting around alone harboring bitterness. Instead, the Father loves you with that same love with which He loved Ruth—desiring that you would serve others just as Ruth did. When you seek to serve others, God will redeem you and equip you for every good work. God's Spirit, your inheritance through Christ your Redeemer, has been poured out on you. His word has been given to you, that you might be adequately prepared for every good work (2 Timothy 3:17). Recognize Him and the goodness of His word today.

"All Scripture is God-breathed and is useful for teaching, rebuking, correcting and training in righteousness, so that the servant of God may be thoroughly equipped for every good work." (2 Timothy 3:16-17)

REFLECT ON THE APPLICATION:

In our story, Ruth clings to the family she found in Naomi and ultimately to her adopted family of Israel. Who is your family and how can you love them in a better way? If you are like Ruth, without a family and a place—let the church be your family and love it and serve it as long as you have breath.

In what ways can you see God's plan for you during this season of your life? Perhaps, you have lost connection to the big picture of God's goodness in the duties of the day but remember how God blessed Ruth for her faithfulness to Naomi. Don't let the potential of bitterness in your widowhood destroy you and instead allow it to motivate you to serve and love others just as Ruth did.

Further study: Read Psalm 90. Before Ruth had a new home with Boaz, the Lord had made Himself her dwelling place. It was He who gave her a heart of servanthood: the willingness to risk losing her life and happiness to love another. It was he who "established the work of her hands." May Psalm 90 be your prayer as you consider the work the Lord has given into your hands today.

Anna, Prophetess and Praise-Giver

God's Rescue Provides Reason for Joy

Now there was a man in Jerusalem called Simeon, who was righteous and devout. He was waiting for the consolation of Israel, and the Holy Spirit was on him. It had been revealed to him by the Holy Spirit that he would not die before he had seen the Lord's Messiah. Moved by the Spirit, he went into the temple courts. When the parents brought in the child Jesus to do for him what the custom of the Law required, Simeon took him in his arms and praised God, saying: "Sovereign Lord, as you have promised, you may now dismiss your servant in peace. For my eyes have seen your salvation, which you have prepared in the sight of all nations: a light for revelation to the Gentiles, and the glory of your people Israel."

The child's father and mother marveled at what was said about him. Then Simeon blessed them and said to Mary, his mother: "This child is destined to cause the falling and rising of many in Israel, and to be a sign that will be spoken against, so that the thoughts of many hearts will be revealed. And a sword will pierce your own soul too."

There was also a prophet, Anna, the daughter of Penuel, of the tribe of Asher. She was very old; she had lived with her husband seven years after her marriage, and then was a widow until she was eighty-four. She never left the temple but worshiped night and day, fasting and praying. Coming up to them at that very moment, she gave thanks to God and spoke about the child to all who were looking forward to the redemption of Jerusalem. (Luke 2:25-38)

Can you imagine this moment? The Messiah—God's rescue for Jerusalem—has finally arrived! Two faithful servants of the Lord, Simeon and Anna, are given the opportunity to see God's plan for salvation with their own eyes. What a reason for praise! Anna responds to what she has overheard with great joy, and she immediately begins to share the good news. But as we read above, it is important to understand that she has not been waiting around idly for a reason to celebrate.

Anna's life is an example of worship, devotion, and service to the One who would never fail her nor abandon her. Her worship, devotion, and service model qualities that should and could be implemented into our lives no matter our age or stage.

"Be strong and courageous. Do not be afraid or terrified because of them, for the Lord your God goes with you; he will never leave you nor forsake you." (Deuteronomy 31:6)

Research the Information...

This passage doesn't reveal much about Anna. The few details that we observe are striking, but they would potentially be lost on us if we didn't go a layer or two deeper. Think about what you know about the author of today's story. You probably remember that Luke wrote both this Gospel and the book of Acts. A physician by vocation, he prepared his narratives with purposeful precision and careful research. With Luke, every detail included in a story is intentional. Every place where he includes less detail is deliberate as well, causing us to pause and engage our imagination when parts are left out.

While Luke does not go into Simeon's lineage, did you notice that he takes time to name Anna as the daughter of Phanuel from the tribe of Asher? Phanuel means "Face of God," and Asher means "blessed." In this passage, we see a threefold blessing in Anna's life, and just as we say of the Lord that He is "holy, holy, holy," we might say of Anna that she is "blessed, blessed, blessed"—commissioned as witness, prophet, and evangelist of the Salvation of the Lord.

First, Luke calls Anna "prophet"—someone whose words tell of God's plan for the salvation of His people. Prophets helped God's people get back on track, pointing to their sin-problem and to the only One who could solve it. Prophets proclaimed the promises of the coming Messiah, the Rescuer and Redeemer, and Israel's future hope. The Lord appointed Anna to speak the promises of His Salvation, bestowing great honor upon this humble but faithful woman. Anna, with Simeon, declared that the Light had come!

Anna was eighty-four years old and had been living in the temple for about sixty-three years. What strikes me as both lovely and challenging is to know that she, while still a young woman, had devoted the rest of her life (after her husband's death) to seeking intimacy with God through worship, prayer, and fasting. From what we can see in the passage, she had not received the same promise as Simeon (that he would see the Lord's salvation before he died). Nonetheless, she had been waiting on the Lord in His house for many decades. Then, when "the fullness of time had come" (Galatians 4:4-7), both in her life and in the course of history, the Lord appointed her as a witness, alongside Simeon, to His Salvation which would come through the baby Jesus brought for presentation that day.

"But when the set time had fully come, God sent his Son, born of a woman, born under the law, to redeem those under

the law, that we might receive adoption to sonship. Because you are his sons, God sent the Spirit of his Son into our hearts, the Spirit who calls out, 'Abba, Father.' So you are no longer a slave, but God's child; and since you are his child, God has made you also an heir." (Galatians 4:4-7)

Anna was also one of the first evangelists; she talked to everyone she knew about the arrival of the One for whom they had been waiting. Even the details of Anna's life were used by the Lord to proclaim His Salvation. Her name, age, the name of her father, and the name of her tribe each communicate something about her witness and evoke vivid reminders of passages of scripture that remind us of God's steady unfolding of His Plan.

God's faithfulness to Anna spurred her on to spread His good news. Though Anna may have never known that her earthly father's name had served as a prophecy, we can clearly see the details of Anna's life. Like Mary (Luke 1:48), Anna, in her widowhood, was a woman "blessed" for all the world to see, for she had seen the "Face of God."

Recognize the Implication...

The "Lord works in mysterious ways!" In spite of the too often over-used nature of that expression, it remains true—maybe you need that reminder today! When we want clarity, God often gives us fog. When we seemingly lose a sense of meaning in life, God surprises us by reminding us that His purpose always includes us. And if we forget all reason for future hope, God impresses upon our minds that we do have reason for a coming hope—Jesus is coming back! I have reason for worship: He knows me, He loves me, He is faithful even in times when we are unfaithful.

"Brothers and sisters, we do not want you to be uninformed about those who sleep in death, so that you do not grieve like the rest of mankind, who have no hope. For we believe that Jesus died and rose again, and so we believe that God will bring with Jesus those who have fallen asleep in him. According to the Lord's word, we tell you that we who are still alive, who are left until the coming of the Lord, will certainly not precede those who have fallen asleep. For the Lord himself will come down from heaven, with a loud command, with the voice of the archangel and with the trumpet call of God, and the dead in Christ will rise first. After that, we who are still alive and are left will be caught up together with them in the clouds to meet the Lord in the air. And so we will be with the Lord forever. Therefore encourage one another with these words." (1 Thessalonians 4:13-18)

Anna, who may no longer have had any family or home, made her dwelling place with her Heavenly Father in His temple. So many Psalms come to mind as I write those words—imagine: these are probably the very words she used as she gave voice to her praise and adoration:

"I will sing of the Lord's great love forever; with my mouth I will make your faithfulness known through all generations... Blessed are those who have learned to acclaim you,

who walk in the light of your presence, Lord. They rejoice in your name all day long; they celebrate your righteousness." (Psalm 89:1, 15-16)

"Lord, you have been our dwelling place throughout all generations."(Psalm 90:1)

"Whoever dwells in the shelter of the Most High will rest in the shadow of the Almighty. I will say of the Lord, "He is my refuge and my fortress, my God, in whom I trust." (Psalm 91:1-2)

"I will sing to the Lord all my life; I will sing praise to my God as long as I live. May my meditation be pleasing to him, as I rejoice in the Lord." (Psalm 104:33-34)

These Psalms and so many others speak of Our Heavenly Father who is our dwelling place, our shelter, our refuge, and the object of our ongoing praise. Maybe these Psalms bring other scripture passages to your mind, or maybe they remind you of the Great Hymns of Faith you have sung since your youth. Allow these words to wash over you, speaking to you of the Lord's goodness and faithfulness as you make your dwelling place in Him, today. Then use them as inspiration and encouragement to faithfully serve and praise God.

REFLECT ON THE APPLICATION...

You may immediately see the fruit, but your example of devotion and spiritual integrity will not return void (see

Isaiah 55:11). The Lord is using you for His good purposes in His perfect timing. How can you continue to grow in intimacy and devotion before the Lord as you wait upon Him in your life?

Anna could not contain the good news that had been revealed to her. What could it look like in your life to share the good news with others? Who in your acquaintance/community might be waiting for these words of life? Pray that the Lord would equip you to tell of His goodness to those who have not heard.

Anna was a great example of staying faithful as a widow and not choosing idleness. How can you use her example to look for opportunities to serve God in His House, the Church?

The Widow's Mite

God's Might Motivates Our Generosity

"Jesus sat down opposite the place where the offerings were put and watched the crowd putting their money into the temple treasury. Many rich people threw in large amounts. But a poor widow came and put in two very small copper coins, worth only a few cents. Calling his disciples to him, Jesus said, "Truly I tell you, this poor widow has put more into the treasury than all the others. They all gave out of their wealth; but she, out of her poverty, put in everything—all she had to live on." (Mark 12:41-44, New Living Translation)

The verses are found in the greater context of a chapter where a lot is going on: Jesus begins with a parable in which He identifies Himself with the Father and predicts His own sacrificial death! He then undergoes testing, by various men in authority from the Sadducees, Pharisees, and Scribes, aimed at catching Him in His words. But Jesus answers each instance in a way that challenges, confounds, astounds, and ultimately silences His questioners. Sadly, they harden their hearts even more against Him. If they had been willing to listen, they would have heard that God (Father, Spirit, and Son-- Jesus Himself) is the only one to whom all glory, honor, authority, and worship is due. The widow of Mark 12 understood this more than all those wise and educated men, and I hope you will too.

Research the Information...

One thing that frequently happens in the Gospels is that people try to trip up Jesus. People heard about the things Jesus did and said and responded in their unbelief with sarcastic remarks and potentially stumping questions. This happens just before our passage for today, where some "wise" men--wise in their own eyes--asked Jesus what they think are difficult questions. Little did they know, however, that they were in the presence of the Ancient of Days--the One who knew all things, including their own hearts even before they asked the questions!

I get this crisp mental image of Jesus as a well-thrown bowling ball sending these tall white-washed pins (Pharisees, Herodians, teachers of the law, Sadducees) flying with Strike after Strike. Can you hear the sound of the ball hitting the pin? Strike! Jesus's words pulled the rug of these men's confidence and arrogance out from under their feet, leaving them scattered in the gutter.

This is the same Jesus who turns over tables in the Temple. He wants all people to come to the Father, and He will not tolerate those who abuse, take advantage of, or create obstacles for others. He drives them out, not with a whip in this case, but with His tongue and leaves them with their ears ringing.

"As he taught, Jesus said, "Watch out for the teachers of the law. They like to walk around in flowing robes and be greeted with respect in the marketplaces, 39 and have the most important seats in the synagogues and the places of honor at banquets. 40 They devour widows' houses and for a show make lengthy prayers. These men will be punished most severely." (Mark 12:38-40).

But then, the final verses of Mark 12 arrive; and Jesus sits, waiting and watching in that quiet moment. A widow, weak and vulnerable to those who might take advantage, comes with all that she has, and she freely gives it. Jesus had just spoken of the ways the very men trying to entrap him earlier in the chapter had cheated widows with their sneaky, manipulative ways. Here, we see a woman who seems untouched by the grasping hands of the power-hungry. Her eyes are on one thing only--her Father, and her gift was freely given.

Little is mentioned of this woman. Even the parallel passage in Luke 21 has no more detail to add. Many rich gifts precede her own; but when she adds her "two cents," they could not have been more profound. She was not trying to get God's attention or to trap Him into giving her something. She wasn't performing to receive glory only He deserved. Her motives were pure, and her actions were rightly subdued.

Her material gift represents much more than material generosity: this widow, trusted that God was able to provide for her and save her—as a result, she gave it all.

"The Lord your God is with you, the Mighty Warrior who saves." (Zephaniah 3:17)

It is also worth noting that Jesus called His disciples to Him to point out the widow. Always wanting to teach and grow His followers, Jesus knew that if He did not point their attention to the faithful widow, His disciples would not have even noticed her and her two cents. Why? Because they were probably focused on what everyone else was focused on—the large gifts given in pompously loud and visible ways. Those who give to God in pride have forgotten that it is the Lord who gave them the ability to gain wealth in the first place.

"You may say to yourself, "My power and the strength of my hands have produced this wealth for me." 18 But remember the Lord your God, for it is he who gives you the ability to produce wealth, and so confirms his covenant, which he swore to your ancestors, as it is today." (Deuteronomy 8:17-18)

And perhaps you even need to be reminded of that today. You might think that your small mite given to God doesn't really matter compared to the more substantial gifts others in the church might give, or even larger gifts other more well-off widows might give. But the beauty of God's economy is fair and straightforward—we are only expected to give out of what we have and not what we do not have. The Widow's "two-cents" were massive in comparison and that fact was not lost on Jesus.

Recognize the Implication...

As I consider this passage, I can't help but think of these words from the Apostle Paul:

"God chose things the world considers foolish in order to shame those who think they are wise. And he chose things that are powerless to shame those who are powerful. God chose things despised by the world, things counted as nothing at all, and used them to bring to nothing what the world considers important. As a result, no one can ever boast in the presence of God." (1 Corinthians 1:27-29)

Jesus didn't come in the way the religious leaders expected: in power, to give them more power over their enemies. No: He came as a small and vulnerable child, welcoming children, championing the weak, the marginalized, the oppressed, and the outcast. He came to those who knew they had need and used them to shame the ones who thought they had it all together. Again remember the words of Paul: from 1 Corinthians:

"Jews demand signs and Greeks look for wisdom, but we preach Christ crucified: a stumbling block to Jews and foolishness to Gentiles, but to those whom God has called, both Jews and Greeks, Christ the power of God and the wisdom of God. For the foolishness of God is wiser than human wisdom, and the weakness of God is stronger than human strength." (1 Corinthians 1:22-24)

The Good News is this: Jesus made himself foolish in the eyes of the world to save those He loves. His gracious plan includes women like the widow of Mark 12 and a widow like you through whom He paints a picture of a very different Kingdom—a Kingdom filled with those who simply and sacrificially give to His Kingdom's work.

Reflect on the Application:

The actions of the poor widow from our passage display her profound gratitude towards the Lord and profoundly pure motivation. Reflect on your life. What has God provided for you? Allow that thought to inspire gratitude in your life, motivating you to love, serve, and give to Him.

The widow from this story also modeled generosity. She communicated the completeness of her trust in her Heavenly Father, giving all that she had materially to show that He deserved all of her worship. Once more from 1 Corinthians 1: 26, Remember, dear brothers and sisters, that few of you were wise in the world's eyes or powerful or wealthy when God called you. What obstacles or fears

Words for the Widow

are you facing today that stand in the way of your ability to give generously to God and His Church?

Further study: Read Matthew 6. Like the widow from Mark 12, put all of your faith and hope in the Mighty King of Heaven, seeking first His Kingdom. What does it look like for you to seek Him and His Kingdom first?

Famine and Feast in Zarephath

A Tale of God's Pursuit and Provision

Then the Lord spoke his word to Elijah, "Go to Zarephath in Sidon and live there. I have commanded a widow there to take care of you."

So Elijah went to Zarephath. When he reached the town gate, he saw a widow gathering wood for a fire. Elijah asked her, "Would you bring me a little water in a cup so I may have a drink?" As she was going to get his water, Elijah said, "Please bring me a piece of bread, too."

The woman answered, "As surely as the Lord your God lives, I have no bread. I have only a handful of flour in a jar and only a little olive oil in a jug. I came here to gather some wood so I could go home and cook our last meal. My son and I will eat it and then die from hunger."

"Don't worry," Elijah said to her. "Go home and cook your food as you have said. But first make a small loaf of bread from the flour you have, and bring it to me. Then cook something for yourself and your son. The Lord, the God of Israel, says, 'That jar of flour will never be empty, and the jug will always have oil in it, until the day the Lord sends rain to the land.'"

So the woman went home and did what Elijah told her to do. And the woman and her son and Elijah had enough food every day. The jar of flour and the jug of oil were never empty, just as the Lord, through Elijah, had promised.

Some time later the son of the woman who owned the house became sick. He grew worse and worse and finally stopped breathing. The woman said to Elijah, "Man of God, what have you done to me? Did you come here to remind me of my sin and to kill my son?"

Elijah said to her, "Give me your son." Elijah took the boy from her, carried him upstairs, and laid him on the bed in the room where he was staying. Then he prayed to the Lord: "Lord my God, this widow is letting me stay in her house. Why have you done this terrible thing to her and caused her son to die?" Then Elijah lay on top of the boy three times. He prayed to the Lord, "Lord my God, let this boy live again!"

The Lord answered Elijah's prayer; the boy began breathing again and was alive. Elijah carried the boy downstairs and gave him to his mother and said, "See! Your son is alive!"

"Now I know you really are a man from God," the woman said to Elijah. "I know that the Lord truly speaks through you!" (1 Kings 17:8-24)

Why do some of the most dreadful circumstances in the Bible seem to fall on widows and orphans? They are already weak, poor, and downtrodden and have already experienced great loss. But they represent an important part of scripture because their stories were recorded for us--to challenge us and increase our faith. As you read today, notice the manner in which our story is retold below, and allow it to sink deeply into your heart.

Research the Information...

Reading over this passage several times, I begin to feel the heaviness the widow of Zarephath must have felt as she sought to engage her daily duties. Though she knew her water, flour, and oil were dwindling, she had no other choice but to go through the daily routine. The routine--Wake up to a parched throat, drag herself from bed, fight off morning hunger pains, fight off despair, and watch her son fade before her eyes, but let him sleep a little longer because she knows his dreams are kinder than their harsh reality.

While many could and even would throw in the towel, her heart hardened, and her mind was more resolved to press on another day, another meal and force her weary legs and arms to repeat yesterday's task one more time. Sticks must be gathered. The fire must be laid. Bread must be baked. We must eat...One Last Time.

Can you feel the conflicted nature of her existence? She has had to accustom herself to the emotions that threaten to consume her in order to go through the motions. Perhaps these daily duties have become her only connection to sanity and maybe even her only reality. The world threatens to pitch into chaos. Only one small thread tenuously connects her to life, ready to snap.

And then it snaps.

Who is this outsider who dares to make so bold a claim on her minimal resources? This Israelite prophet to whom so much has supposedly been revealed! Doesn't he know that she is a widow and that all has been taken from her already? How dare he tell her "not to be afraid?" Maybe his promises sounded hollow to her. Maybe she returned to her mind-numbing motions, her coping mechanism to ward off the yawning abyss that stretched before her.

She sets the fire. She serves the water. She scrapes the bottom of her flour jar, tilting her jug almost upside down to apply the oil and pat out a cake of bread. She places the bread over the heat, and the smell of this final morsel causes her stomach to quiver perhaps even bringing tears to her eyes. She cannot deny that she is desperately hungry, no matter how she tries to bury herself in her responsibilities, she knows well her desperate state. She turns away from the prophet to hide her tears, turning back to the motions of duty. Her muscle-memory kicks in—no deep thoughts needed just do what you have to do. So, she scrapes the bottom of the jar once more...

But wait, what is this? Had she misjudged? There was enough for another measure of a flour... another trickle of oil... A second cake makes it to the small fire. The little loaf makes it into the skin-and-bone hands of her son, whose eyes, already enlarged in his hunger, grow enormous as he watches his mother scrape a third loaf's worth of flour and still more oil together.

And so, it continues for many days. The widow, the prophet, and her family eat for many days. The gnawing pain in her belly becomes a memory. Her son begins to put weight back on; he looks less frail. She sees color return to his face and a sparkle of playfulness to his eyes. The thread has been woven afresh and anew that connects the daily routine of her life and genuine hope once more. She scrapes up her flour, trickles her oil, and laughs for the first time in months as she asks herself is this really happening?

Then just as quickly as joy and hope returned, it happened. Her son's life begins to wane once more. She watches helplessly, perhaps even silently berating herself for having allowed herself to hope again because it is more painful now. Wake, watch, scrape, bake...but this time the motions don't bridge her to new hope. Her son dies, shredding her faith, laying bare her heart. She feels mocked, and in return, she mocks the "man of God" who has entered her house. With no strength left and no reason left to live, she can no longer cope. She has hit rock bottom.

And that's precisely where the Lord meets her.

Recognize the Implication...

The widow of Zarephath, compared to the widows of our stories so far seems to be in a different place both emotionally and spiritually. Each of them has endured hardship, loss, abandonment, and neglect. But in each of the other cases, we see women working out their faith: their understanding of justice, mercy, salvation, worship, generosity. The previous stories of widows finding their place and purpose seem to move rapidly to redemptive themes, or they highlight some attractive character trait. What is striking in this passage is that this woman begins with no apparent relationship with or understanding of Yahweh--the One God of Israel. Understandably, she is reluctant to take a risk and trust the man of God and his words to her. She faces not one but TWO life-threatening challenges within the course of the short narrative.

What can we take from this? Was the Lord particularly harsh with her? Or maybe, which I believe is more accurate, we are seeing the Lord's relentless pursuit of this unbelieving and broken widow. She was parched, but not only for water; she was hungry, but not merely for bread.

Her desperate heart needed more than the presence of more flour, oil, sticks, a fire, and an earthly son. What she really needed most was the unfailing provision of a Heavenly Father.

When the story starts, she was desperate for sure, but she was actually way more desperate than she knew. Her physical hunger paled in comparison to her spiritual need. Even in the challenges the Lord allowed in her life, He pursued her to the point of life-giving faith, providing bread and water to renew her physically, her son's life to support her emotionally, and words of truth spoken by the man of God to restore her spiritually.

REFLECT ON THE APPLICATION…

Have you, like the widow of Zarephath, been struggling to trust the Lord's provision for your needs, physically, emotionally, and/or spiritually? Whether your answer is yes or no, go to Him now with all your needs and all your worship, thankful for all He has done—and will continue to do—in your life. Feast on Him: the Bread of Life.

What is the hardest thing for you to trust the Lord with right now? Did you notice how the Lord moved Elijah into the most sensitive and painful areas of the widow's life, pushing into them as He pursued her heart? Consider inviting a friend into this area of struggle. Ask them to pray for you. Allow them to speak words of truth and provision (as Elijah did for the widow of Zarephath) into this area of your life then press on, waiting for your Heavenly Father to provide a miracle.

The Widow from Nain

Christ, Incarnate, Displays His Compassion & His Power

Soon afterward, Jesus went to a town called Nain, and his disciples and a large crowd went along with him. As he approached the town gate, a dead person was being carried out—the only son of his mother, and she was a widow. And a large crowd from the town was with her. When the Lord saw her, his heart went out to her and he said, "Don't cry."

Then he went up and touched the coffin they were carrying him on, and the bearers stood still. He said, "Young man, I say to you, get up!" The dead man sat up and began to talk, and Jesus gave him back to his mother.

They were all filled with awe and praised God. "A great prophet has appeared among us," they said. "God has come to help his people." This news about Jesus spread throughout Judea and the surrounding country. (Luke 7:11-17)

As we look at this story, we can see that the Lord Jesus Christ fulfilled all the law and the prophets in His actions. Reaching out in a display of Resurrection power, He proved He was the greater "Elijah" and would minister to the poor and oppressed, the widow, and the orphan. Jesus would leave behind a "double portion" of His Spirit upon His disciples after His ascension. They, in turn, would take up His mantle, like Elisha, continuing to spread the glorious truth of God's provision through His Son, doing mighty works in His name and for His glory.

Research the Information...

Often throughout this series of narratives, we have seen how the Lord communicated something of Himself and His purposes through widows. We have seen Him weave into His redemptive tapestry the threads of widows who were foreigners; widows who were oppressed; and widows who had lost their sons. In His word, the Lord even uniquely uses Nabal's widow and a metaphor of widowhood to challenge King David, His anointed Old Testament forerunner. Through these widows' narratives and the careful instructions the Lord gave to His people Israel in the Old Testament and the Church in the New Testament—we see clearly the Lord's tender and generous heart toward widows.

We see His heart most clearly in the person of Jesus Christ who says to this widow, "Don't Cry." His heart is clearly overflowing with compassion for her. Think of what it would have meant to see Him at this moment as if He was saying this to you face-to-face—Don't Cry!

Then, He unleashes His awesome power. Filled with human compassion but also fully God, Jesus makes everything in the material and spiritual world obey Him, so that even death must walk back at his Word and because of His authority. Even Elijah and Elisha and the other prophets did not have the same authority. They wielded authority, yes--but if you have read the chapters carefully where these prophets interceded for the sons who had died, you will have noticed that they had to pray to the Lord asking Him to restore life. What happened in this story? Jesus authoritatively stated: "I say to you, get up!"

This is not an everyday, run-of-the-mill occurrence. This experience puts the fear of God into those who witnessed it. And it inspired the only, right response: praise to God and proclamation of the good news to those who had not heard or seen the works they had witnessed. God had, in fact, come to His people that day, in the person and power of His Son, Jesus Christ.

RECOGNIZE THE IMPLICATION...

Did you notice the words used by Luke--that "This news about Jesus spread throughout Judea and the surrounding country?" Does it remind you of another book Luke wrote? In Acts 1:8, Jesus sends His disciples out to proclaim the good news of His coming: "But you will receive power when the Holy Spirit comes upon you. And you will be my witnesses, telling people about me everywhere--in Jerusalem, throughout Judea, in Samaria, and to the ends of the earth."

The gospel of Jesus Christ is this: God loved us *so much* that He sent His Son who died, conquering death for all time by His Resurrection. By His Spirit, God has bestowed power upon you--a double portion of Himself. The Spirit is a seal and a pledge: you are His; He is going to return for you to bring you home someday! Drink deeply today of His compassion. Know that the power of the Resurrection is yours in Christ, for you are united to Him forever by His Spirit. Let this be your comfort today, proclaiming it to your heart, aloud, and to anyone else who might need to hear it: "I am HIS, and HE is mine!" So, Don't Cry!

REFLECT ON THE APPLICATION...

Further Study: Ephesians 1:13-14 (NLT) connects solidly with our passage and takeaways for today:

"So it is with you. When you heard the true teaching—the Good News about your salvation—you believed in Christ. And in Christ, God put his special mark of ownership on you by giving you the Holy Spirit that he had promised. That Holy Spirit is the guarantee that we will receive what God promised for his people until God gives full freedom to those who are his—to bring praise to God's glory.

Consider memorizing the two verses above.

How has it impacted you to read these stories? How did the story of the compassion of our Loving Savior and Lord toward the widow of Nain strike you? This narrative was a mere ten lines long—and yet *so* profound! Spend a moment and write a ten-line narrative of God's compassion toward you. Reflect on His goodness and praise His name.

What is your first response to hearing good news? If you're like me, you want to shout it and share it with everyone you come across. The news of Jesus Christ, the One who had the power to conquer death, spread like wildfire in this story. Seek out opportunities to tell of the good news you have found in Him (perhaps using the narrative you wrote above to help you bear witness to His compassion and power).

www.ingramcontent.com/pod-product-compliance
Lightning Source LLC
Chambersburg PA
CBHW060851050426
42453CB00008B/942